TIDEWATER

The Chesapeake Bay in Photographs

STEPHEN R. BROWN

No part of this book may be reproduced without
the written permission of Stephen R. Brown.

Photography © 2010 Stephen R. Brown
Design and maps by Jessica Warren | www.heyjess.com
Text by June Brown and Caitlin Brown
Edited by Jeffrey Wilkes and Tod Ragsdale

Published by Stephen R. Brown Studio, Washington, D.C.
www.srbphoto.com | srb@srbphoto.com | (202) 667-1965
www.chesapeakebayphotobook.com

CONTENTS

INTRODUCTION 5

THE EASTERN SHORE 7

Chesapeake Bay Bridge 8
Chestertown 12
Kent Narrows 16
Wye River 18
St. Michaels 22
Miles River 26

TILGHMAN ISLAND 29

Knapps Narrows 30
Skipjack "Rebecca Ruark" 38

THE CHOPTANK RIVER 45

Choptank River 46
Dun's Cove 48
Oxford 50
Cutts & Case Shipyard 54
Oxford Boatyard 58
Log Canoes 60

THE LOWER BAY 65

Lower Bay 66
Smith Island 70
Chickahominy River 72

THE WESTERN SHORE 81

Solomon's Island 82
Jug Bay 86
Herring Bay 90
Deale 94
Agriculture 96
West River 98
Annapolis 100
Baltimore 106
Susquehanna River 108

L'ESCARGOT 112

INTRODUCTION

To those of you unfamiliar with the Chesapeake Bay, it is a 200-mile long estuary bordered by Virginia and Maryland. At its navigable narrowest, it is two miles across, and at its widest, 30 miles. It is fed by the Susquehanna River at the north and merges with the Atlantic Ocean at the south. Another 150 rivers and streams flow into the Bay at various points. The area is probably both as historic and contemporary a region as you will find in the Americas. New York, Philadelphia, and Washington, D.C. are all within 60 miles. The larger towns on the Bay - Oxford, Solomon's, St. Michaels, Annapolis and Baltimore - were the major "ports" and "points of taxation" during Colonial times. Sixty years ago, the residents of once remote Smith Island were still speaking English with an Elizabethan accent. Since then, the Bay Bridge has been built and the Eastern Shore is no longer so remote. In fact, Smith Island was recently featured in a series of Internet advertisements.

John Smith, our first and legendary real estate salesman, (and Lothario…) wrote, "that abundance of fish, lying so thick… we attempted to catch them with a frying pan." Today the Chesapeake still manages a healthy fish population but the whole ecosystem is in serious trouble. In the late 20th and early 21st centuries, 14,000 watermen worked the Bay for oysters. Oysters, which serve as natural water filters, cleaned the Bay every three days. Today the oyster population is significantly smaller and so their natural filtering is non-existent. .

My family and I have been boating and photographing the Chesapeake Bay for thirty-plus years and as frequently as 100 days per year. I have on more than one occasion convinced magazine editors to send me to the Bay on assignment. I have hitched helicopter and small plane rides when I could, and the Coast Guard and state rangers have been kind enough to bring me along as they do their work. The great trick of photography is making images of what you love.

Exploring the Bay is exhilarating and forgiving. When the weather is rough, the proximity of shallow water (and there is plenty of that) makes for a quick anchorage. Its 11,000 miles of shoreline provide plenty of cozy anchorages. We have made great friends at the many marinas where we have spent a night or two to freshen up. Encounters with tidal flow and the insane humor of the Knapp's Narrows bridge tenders keep the heart racing and our boat handling skills fresh.

Ever an optimist, I would say there is some progress on the Bay. Rockfish are back, Ospreys now occupy every available piling, and marinas use technology to ensure that boating wastes are recovered. However, we are loving the Bay to death. I hope these images will inspire you to explore, enjoy and protect this pristine natural estuary.

The Pride of Baltimore maneuvers into dock during "Downrigging Weekend" held every Fall at Chestertown, MD.

THE EASTERN SHORE

CHESAPEAKE BAY BRIDGE

The Bay Bridge at 4.3 miles long was a technological *tour de force* when it opened in 1952. It is high enough at 186 feet so that commercial shipping can get to Baltimore, a major Eastern seaboard port. On weekend nights, the Bay Bridge is awash in traffic heading both to the Eastern Shore and farther on to Ocean City and Rehoboth. Under the Bridge, a steady stream of cargo carriers, cruise lines, work and pleasure boats make their way about the Bay.

Because of its unique architecture (seven different spans) and location, the Bridge has become both a symbol for Bay preservationists and its own tourist destination. There is a yearly "Bay Bridge Walk" to support area conservation which is an opportunity to see the Bay from a unique perspective.

CHESTERTOWN

Chestertown, Maryland is a long day's sail up the Chester River from the Bay. As in colonial days, it is a major agricultural center for the Eastern Shore. Prior to the American Revolution, it was also a "Royal Port" and therefore a center of British taxation. Today the town is still well known for resisting large corporate entities and displays a continuing spirit of resistance, celebrating Independence Day with a "Tea Party" (p. 15). Fittingly, it is also the main base for the Sultana Project. Centerpiece of the Project is the *Sultana*, a re-creation of a Colonial British Tax Ship.

Pictured here is *Downrigging Weekend* where several other Tall Ships dock at the Town Dock for a Fall Festival. The Sultana Project and weekend events like these provide a link to the rich maritime heritage of the Chester River. The Sultana sails the Bay ten months a year, primarily visiting ports along the Bay and teaching school children the Bay's history and environment. There are many arts and crafts shops in Chestertown along with fine dining and a beautiful waterfront seen in these pictures.

KENT NARROWS

Kent Island is the largest on the Chesapeake Bay. Crowded on the northern end with beach traffic and condos, the southern part has abundant wildlife refuges, secluded coves and great views of the sun as it rises and sets. On the eastern side of the island is a waterway which connects the Chester River with Eastern Bay. It is called the "Narrows" for good reason. The tidal race runs quickly under the drawbridge, making navigation very difficult. The difficulty of this passage and the ensuing shouting between boats is always a source of much amusement at the restaurants and bars along the waterway.

With multiple packinghouses in operation in the latter half of the Twentieth Century, the Narrows was the heart of the seafood industry. Today numerous seafood restaurants are all that remain. The waterway is regularly dredged to prevent it from silting closed. Make sure you study your charts and bring a horn!

WYE RIVER

The Wye River joins the Miles River near its mouth at Eastern Bay and is easily accessible from the main Bay or from Kent Narrows. Gracing the shores of the Wye River are manor houses and estates, one of which boasts an alluring private lighthouse (right) as you enter the river at Bennett Point. After you pass the point, the Wye splits into two forks, the Wye East and the western fork. The two branches enfold Wye Island, a wildlife refuge. The Wye itself affords safe, lovely anchorages, such as Shaw Bay just off the main river. A serene and rather remote setting, the Wye River region attracted the world's attention in 1998 when it served as a fitting venue for the Middle East Peace Talks hosted by President Bill Clinton, with Benjamin Netanyahu, Prime Minister of Israel, and Yasser Arafat, Chairman of the Palestinian Authority, in attendance.

ST. MICHAELS

St. Michaels became known as "the town that fooled the British" during the War of 1812 when the townsfolk dimmed the lights and hung lanterns in the trees, sparing them from a direct attack by the British. Their forebears had settled in St. Michaels nearly 150 years earlier, establishing an Episcopal Parish that gave the town its name. Today St. Michaels is home to the Chesapeake Bay Maritime Museum, which boasts skipjacks and other historic bay vessels, the old drawbridge from Knapps Narrows at Tilghman Island, and the lighthouse that once marked Hooper Strait, the entrance to Tangier Sound. Keepers of the beacon could not live at the lighthouse with their families, used water collected from the roof's rain gutters for drinking, bathing and cooking, and availed themselves of an outhouse located on the lighthouse's deck. Many of the museum's displays deal with waterfowling and environmental issues. There is a large woodworking community working to restore the many boats they have managed to keep for preservation.

MILES RIVER

The Miles River, a tributary of Eastern Bay, provides access to St. Michaels and other towns on the Eastern Shore. Besides access to St. Michaels, the Miles River affords lovely, safe anchorages to boaters, whether just outside the town of St. Michaels or on the smaller creeks off the Miles River, such as Leeds Creek. The Miles River is an excellent vantage point for watching sailboat and log canoe races on the river. It is also home to two species of swans—the Tundra Swan in the winter and the Mute Swan year round—which are not shy in greeting boats at anchorage on the Miles. In fact, you may want to keep your fingers in the boat lest they attract a quick nibble.

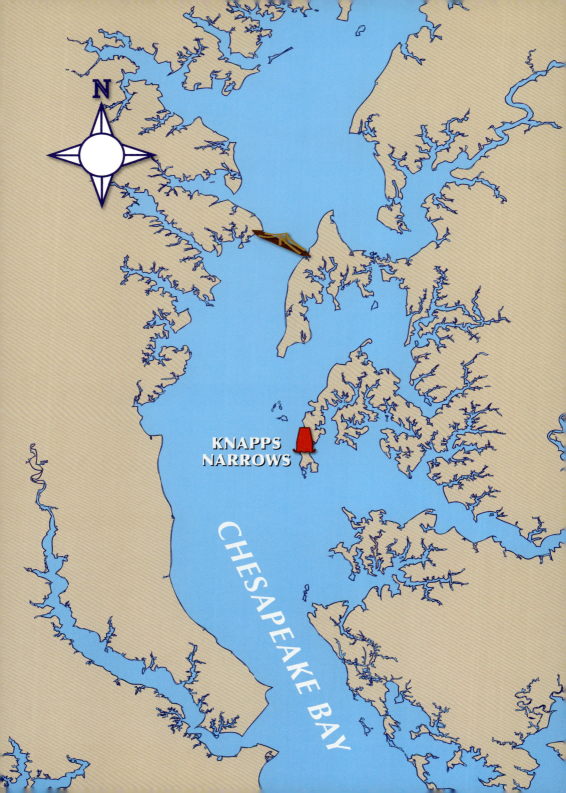

TILGHMAN ISLAND

KNAPPS NARROWS

Knapps Narrows on Tilghman Island is perhaps the most interesting waterfront on the Bay. A dredged channel called the Narrows runs from the Chesapeake to the Choptank River. It is used by many pleasure and commercial boats trying to save time. They have to get through the drawbridge, which is also the island's only road so the bridge does not open for long. If you take a seat at one of the bars or restaurants nearby the bridge, you'll get a view of the antics of boaters trying to make it under the bridge. Knapps Narrows and the Kent Island Narrows are the two places on the Bay where a tidal chart and good planning are absolutely necessary to the boater.

Thirty years ago, the Federal government put in a sewer system on Tilghman Island and since then the development of the area has been amazingly fast. New "Chesapeake Bay-Themed" developments are springing up every year (p. 36). There are a number of hotels and lodges which serve fishermen and hunters and are active all year long.

REBECCA RUARK

A number of determined Captains like Wade Murphy still manage to keep their skipjacks in pristine condition. Murphy bought the boat and immediately had to rebuild her from stem to stern. I have had the opportunity to go out with the Rebecca as Captain Murphy and crew tried for oysters. We got $85.00 worth for the entire crew. A more successful venture was for the State of Maryland as we harvested "spat" (baby oyster or larvae... p. 42-43) and moved it around the Bay in the hopes of restarting the oyster population.

The primary cargo of the skipjacks today are tourists, wedding parties and corporate outings. Captain Murphy still brings the Rebecca out oystering during the winter months. He is so determined that several years ago, the boat sank in high winds that would have driven another skipper into port. Within 24 hours, he had started a fund to rebuild the Rebecca which allowed him to bring it to its now pristine condition.

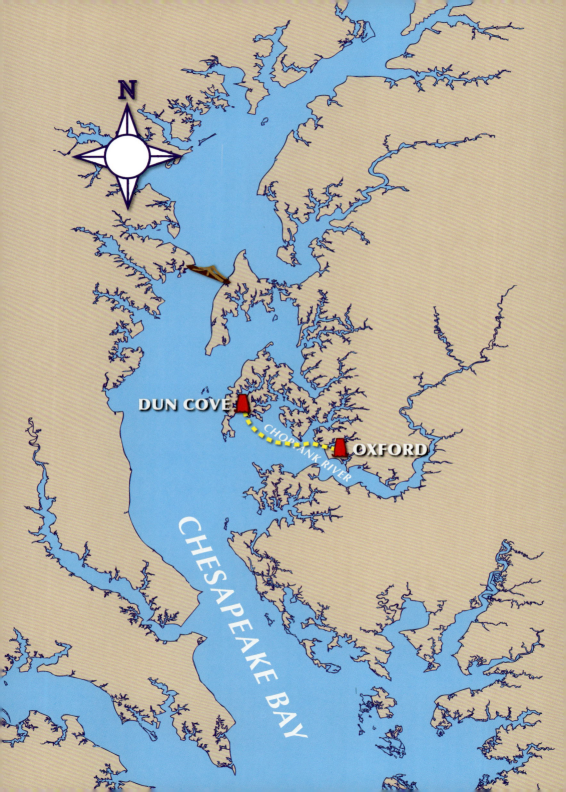

THE CHOPTANK RIVER

CHOPTANK RIVER

The Choptank River is a major tributary of the Bay and the essence of the Eastern Shore. Rivers like the Tred Avon, and waterways like Broad Creek and Dun's Cove are a boater's delight. Quick access to cozy anchorage is everywhere. Entering the Choptank gives you water access to Oxford, Cambridge and St. Michael's and finally to La Trappe Creek. The river affords captivating views of all manner of workboats and pleasure craft on the water and lovely estates along the shore. Numerous creeks branch off the main river, with their own memorable sights and safe anchorages. Osprey, Bald Eagles and Great Blue Herons glide and swoop by, and it's easy to imagine early settlers to the region basking in its richness.

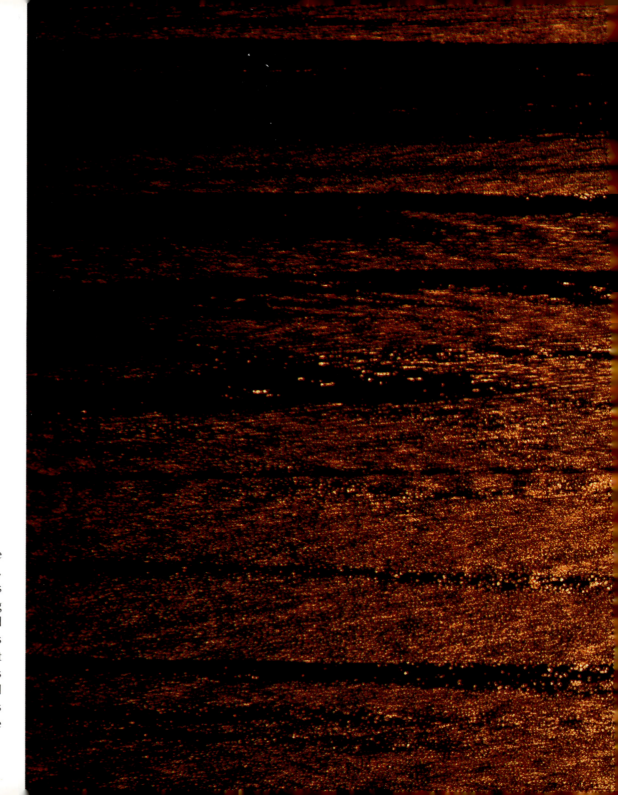

DUN'S COVE

Dun's Cove is a small creek on the eastern side of Tilghman Island which is bordered by a farm. For the boater, it is a "find" and, while not a secret, is difficult enough to reach that it's rarely crowded. It is large and open enough to get out in a dinghy and explore. It's typical of many of the small creeks in this area, and you'll see heron and deer on the shoreline. Get to bed early as you'll be awakened before dawn by the sounds of crabbers working the cove.

OXFORD

Oxford, one of the earliest seaports on the Bay, has retained its quiet and historic charm. It's a haven from the hustle and bustle of city life and our most frequent stop on the Bay. The Oxford Ferry - the oldest private ferry in the United States - carries cars and bicyclists across the river. The Tred Avon Yacht Club runs daily sailing camps and weekend sailing races. There are lovely sunset views along the river as sailboats, crabbers and motor yachts round Number Two Buoy and sail into anchor along the Strand, the town promenade.

Take a short walk around town and you find yourself browsing about Cutts and Case Boat Builders where they still build and maintain wooden yachts. Sailing up river you can anchor in front of the many mansions along the river's edge. The Robert Morris Inn is named after the financier of the American Revolution.

CUTTS & CASE SHIPYARD

I've never seen a boat I didn't like! So a visit to Cutts and Case is, to me, a pilgrimage to the Promised Land. Here they still build wooden boats and have developed a patented construction process to modernize wooden boat building. It is the oldest shipyard on the Bay and the heart of Chesapeake maritime history.

Years back, if you were lucky, Eddie Cutts might join you on your walk through the Marina all the while sketching his ideas on any piece of wood available. While on assignment for a magazine, I convinced him to race us up the Tred Avon River with one of his sleek and narrow sailboats. The shipyard has a museum/showroom which is open to the public, and classic boats like *Foto* - the photo platform for the legendary Stanley and Morris Rosenfeld Photography - are on display.

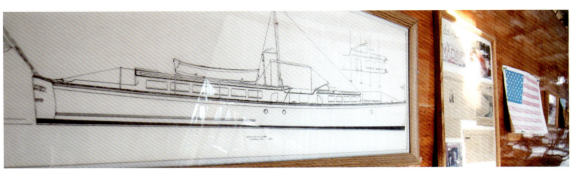

OXFORD BOATYARD

Oxford, despite pressure to rezone its maritime commercial area for condominiums and townhouses, has somehow protected its boating industry. Truly a yachtsman's paradise, the deep Tred Avon River allows transatlantic vessels to stop and have maintenance done while their owners enjoy the quiet tranquility of the town. Over the years, I have found it a wealth of photographic opportunity.

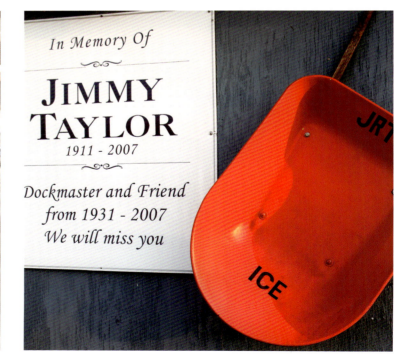

In Memory Of

Jimmy Taylor

1911 – 2007

Dockmaster and Friend
from 1931 – 2007
We will miss you

LOG CANOES

These gangly wooden craft have been raced in this area for the past 150 years. It is said that the design was based on native Indian craft and that they were originally used to deliver oysters. Their narrow width makes that seem impractical. The 18 boats that make up the fleet are all in the National Register of Historic Places and they always make for wonderful pictures.

In a stiff wind, the boardsmen run up 12-15 foot boards from side to side to balance the craft. A sudden gust or a large wake can capsize these graceful craft. Signing on to the crew of a log canoe is a full-time commitment for the summer. The fleet moves their racing around the Bay relying on logistical support from local yacht clubs.

THE LOWER BAY

SMITH ISLAND

You can only get there by boat, whether a ferry from Crisfield on the mainland or smaller craft from the main Bay or Tangier Sound. If you are too far out in the main Bay or visibility is low, you may cruise by Smith Island without realizing it. This collection of small islands is predominantly low, salt marsh with an elevation of less than four feet! Two of the three towns, Ewell and Rhodes Point, are within walking distance of each other, but the third, Tylerton, is only accessible by boat.

Captain John Smith first mapped the island in 1608 although the island is named for Henry Smith of Jamestown who was granted 1,000 acres there in 1679. Today's residents speak a local dialect similar to that of the West Country of England. They make their living mainly from the surrounding waters, which Captain Smith described as "having such an abundance of fish... that he and his crew, lacking nets, attempted to catch them with frying pans!"

NORTHERN NECK

The Tidewater Virginia peninsulas known as the Northern Neck and the Middle Peninsula are relatively remote compared to the Upper Bay. Upstream stretches of the York and Rappahannock Rivers are seemingly untouched by human habitation since the native Indian tribes populated the area. This area of the Bay contains a number of historic fishing villages where Chesapeake watermen still harvest fish, crabs, eels and oysters depending on the season.

As this is the home of the earliest settlements, you can visit the birthplace of both George Washington and Robert E. Lee, who were born on Northern Neck plantations. Reedsville, one of the oldest and most traditional towns, has a fishermen's museum. It is also the home of the Menhaden Fleet, which plies the lower bay in search of these tiny bait fish. The Coast Guard's mission today is as much law enforcement as it is life-saving. They patrol these waters and maintain lighthouses like the Wolf Trap Light all year long.

CHICKAHOMINY RIVER

The Chickahominy River flows into the James River near the mouth of the Bay and is unique for its Bald Cypress trees which are unusual this far north. This is shallow water boating and I have only seen a few adventurous deep draft cruisers in this area. These next few pages are the result of a few days' photography. The Cypress Trees are home to Bald Eagles and Bass. The Cypress Tree's unique root system makes for striking photography. The aerials show the meandering channels that make up the waterway, which is now part of the Chesapeake Bay Gateways Network and the John Smith Trail.

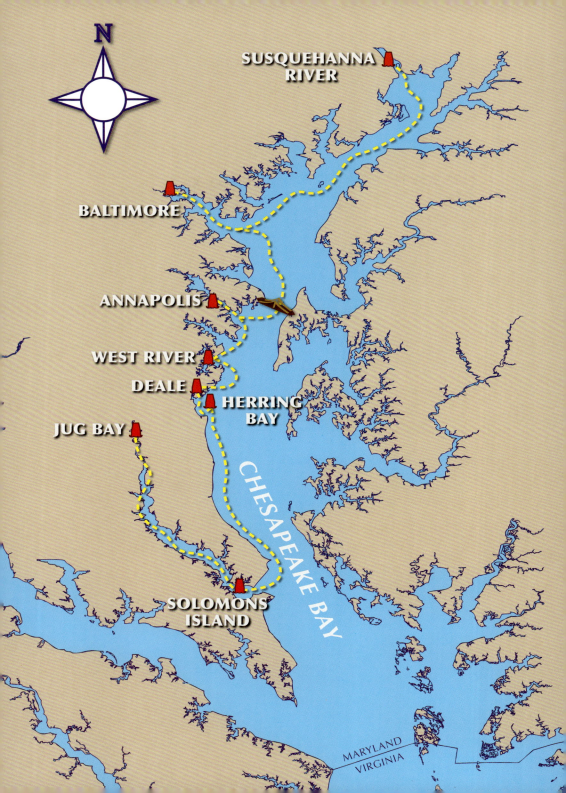

THE WESTERN SHORE

SOLOMON'S ISLAND

The island is a two-mile strip jutting into the mouth of the Patuxent River where it joins the Chesapeake Bay. It is home to the Calvert County Museum. 14,000 people were employed in the town at the height of the oyster boom, and "Solomon's" became synonymous with both seafood and boat building. During WWII it was the center of a relatively large wartime effort designing Naval craft. The town is just across the river from the Patuxent Naval Base, so it's rocking all year long!

During WWII, several captured German vessels were anchored in the deep river, and there's rumor that just west of the Bridge there's a captured German submarine, which was sunk so U.S. Naval Divers can practice. There are a number of creeks and rivers which make for great anchorage west of the town.

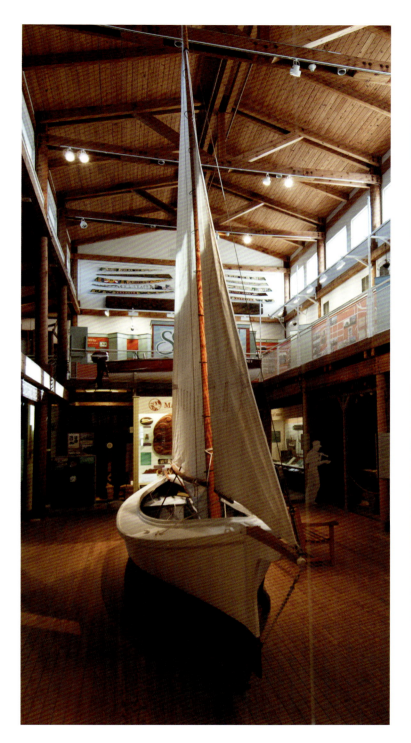

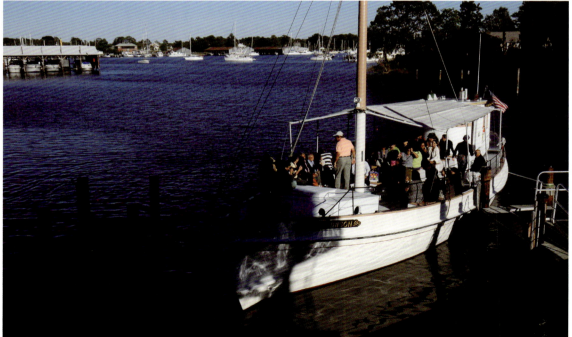

JUG BAY

"Buy land, they're not making it anymore."
— Mark Twain

Maryland's legendary comptroller Louis L. Goldstein initiated many controversial purchases buying prime properties and turning them into historical and recreational areas. He always quoted Twain to justify his sometimes costly purchases, which more often than not proved to be clever deals.

Jug Bay, formerly a private estate, is now an extensive environmental refuge along the Patuxtent River, which 100 miles farther south flows into the Bay at Solomon's Island. This is a series of images I have taken at dawn and dusk from the rental canoes that are available at the headquarters. The deep river is home to eagles, herons and reedbirds (p. 88), and the historic farmhouse can be seen in the background as the ducks take off (p. 89).

HERRING BAY

Herrington Harbour South at the southern tip of Herring Bay is home port for our sailboat L'Escargot and launch point for sailing and photography. The Herring Bay marine authorities usually ignore my occasional aerial and photographic hi-jinks. For this picture we mounted two remotely triggered cameras on the spreaders of the sailboat "Belle Marie". The Osprey on page 92 is just one of a family that has grown in size. Tundra Swans choose Herring Bay to gather in winter. Most boats bound for Herrington Harbour or Deale make for the Number Two Buoy just before sunset and swing into the channel or anchorage near the southern portion of Herring Bay.

DEALE

A number of environmentally conscious entrepreneurs have entered the Marina field. In the early 90s, Steuart Chaney joined several marinas together and created a high-tech marine center, featuring fiberglass shops, fine woodwork, canvas, rigging, engine work, large lifts and year-round storage. Herrington Harbour North is home to a number of historic buildings Chaney has moved here from around the Bay. Deale also continues to be a center for charter, sport fishing and hunting. And it has been the home for many years to the famous Happy Harbor Inn.

AGRICULTURE

I have had the occasion to fly with the door off in a helicopter as I've done these maritime assignments. As we cruise over land preparing for another watery approach, you can actually smell the richness of the farmland from 300 feet above. Any trip to the Bay involves countless scenic fields and my never-ending project: tobacco barns… but that's another book. The Annapolis through Solomon's corridor travels through not only agriculture but also some beautiful equestrian farms. I try to avoid the distraction of car shows, late season corn, and tractor pulls; but sometimes it's hard not to just stop and enjoy the rich diversity of the Bay region.

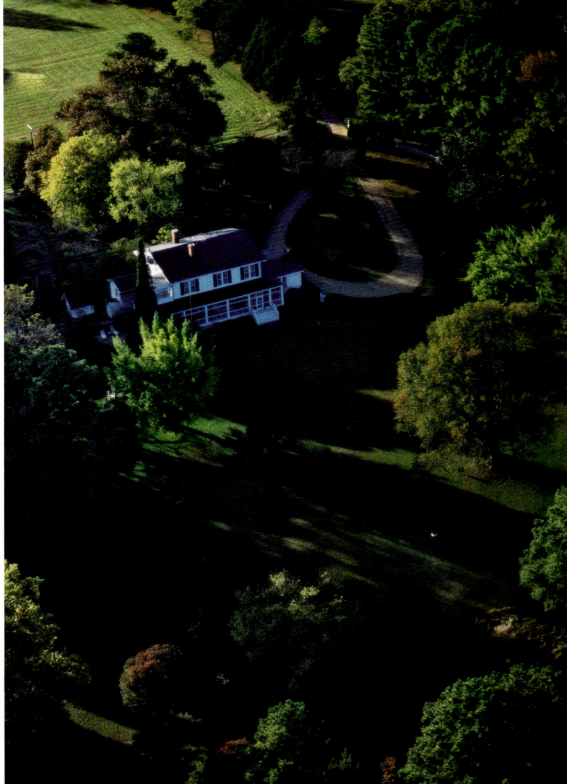

WEST RIVER

The West River Sailing Association conveniently stages many of their races right out of Galesville, Maryland, so I often drive down and watch from the dock. I am always impressed when the skippers of these expensive boats risk serious damage in the daring pre-race maneuvers.

You can also anchor right off the town of Galesville, Maryland to take advantage of a number of fine restaurants and then sail back out the River toward the Bay and anchor in the nearby Rhode River where the swimming is excellent.

ANNAPOLIS

It is the yachting capital of the eastern United States, the home of the Naval Academy and the capital of the State of Maryland. I suspect because of the capital's proximity to the Bay, Maryland has one of the most progressive environmental programs in the United States. On any Sunday, it's hard to see the water for the boats as yacht clubs and marinas host racing boats of every variety and vintage.

Located near the Bay Bridge, Annapolis is also a mere twenty-seven miles from Washington, DC and Baltimore. Annapolis hosts a Maritime Museum and a number of sailing schools and art galleries devoted to Bay History. "Ego Alley" (p. 103, right) is the site where you can watch new boat owners strut their stuff. The entire downtown is a registered National Historic Landmark.

BALTIMORE

Baltimore is the largest port on the Chesapeake and home to cruise lines, harbor pilots and a huge international shipping facility, making sailing a small craft a challenge. As is obvious in this picture, the residents of Charm City enjoy the proximity of the Bay and the Inner Harbor area is much influenced by the city's rich maritime past.

The *Pride of Baltimore* (below) is a sailing reproduction of an 1812 Baltimore Clipper, the kind of vessel that participated in the Chesapeake Campaign during the War of 1812. Over its working life, the *Pride of Baltimore* sailed over 200,000 nautical miles and visited over 200 ports in 37 countries, in North, South, and Central America, Europe, and the Far East. Baltimore is also the host of the *Round The World Sailing Race*, and watching these amazing racing boats come down the Bay is quite thrilling.

SUSQUEHANNA RIVER

The Susquehanna River is the main tributary of the Chesapeake Bay. Stretching down from New York State through Pennsylvania, it transforms into the Bay at Havre de Grace, Maryland. The River accounts for approximately fifty percent of the Bay's water. The size of the Chesapeake Bay Watershed is approximately 64,000 square miles, and it interconnects with some 100,000 other streams and rivers. So Delaware, Maryland, New York, Pennsylvania, Virginia, and West Virginia have formed the Chesapeake Bay Program to try to make information available to the 17 million people who call the Chesapeake Bay Watershed home. On these pages, you can see the railroad tracks that parallel the Susquehanna River at Harrisburg and then turn south past power plants and waterfalls towards Havre de Grace and the entry to the Bay.

L'ESCARGOT

A 1976 thirty-two foot Bristol sailboat has kept us safe on our journeys around the Bay. She draws five feet and, once happily stuck in the Bay mud, requires a powerful towboat to pull her out. A "classic yacht," she is being rebuilt this year with a more powerful engine, new hatches and a few more amenities.